T·H·

CH

T·H·E B·E·S·T O·F
CHOCOLATE

GARAMOND

First published by Garamond Ltd, Publishers
Strode House, 44–50 Osnaburgh Street, London NW1 3ND

Copyright © Garamond Ltd, Publishers 1990

ISBN 1–85583–056–6

Illustrations by Madeleine David

Printed and bound in UK by MacLehose and Partners Ltd.
Typeset by Bookworm Ltd.

CONTENTS

INTRODUCTION

Chocolate is a universal favourite, associated with indulgences and romance around the world. Ancient Mexican Aztecs are credited with its discovery, and their influence is still seen today in the use of chocolate in savoury Mexican and Spanish dishes.

This luscious confection is made from cocoa beans with varying amounts of sugar and fat, and comes in a wide range of colours and flavours. Milk chocolate, as its name implies, has had milk added during production. Plain chocolate is sold as either the lighter sweetened variety or the darker bitter variety. For fine desserts and delicate sweets buy couverture chocolate, available from delicatessens and some of the larger supermarkets. Avoid chocolate-flavoured cake covering for all the recipes in this book; it is not a true chocolate.

Chocolate's link with romance was probably established because it contains caffeine, which gives a quick burst of energy, as well as a natural amphetamine called phenylethylamine. Scientists say our brain produces this chemical in varying amounts, and if our body contains more than normal levels we experience rapidly changing emotions ... just like being in love!

Dieters are well aware of the high calories in chocolate: plain chocolate has 525 per 100 grams (4 oz), while milk chocolate has 530 for the same amount. Yet, there are a few nutritional benefits to chocolate, as it contains small amounts of protein, carbohydrate, iron, potassium and calcium. In fact, a 100–125 grams (4 oz) bar of milk chocolate contains almost half the daily recommended amount of calcium for grown-ups.

Carob, made from the pod of a tree often grown in the Mediterranean, is a popular health-food alternative to chocolate because it does not contain caffeine. Buy it in bar form from health food shops, and be sure to read the label because it is often flavoured rather than plain.

Take great care when melting chocolate because it can easily burn. All the recipes in this book recommend either melting the chocolate in a liquid, or melting it in a bowl over simmering water.

CHURROS Y CHOCOLATE

400 grams (14 oz) plain flour
300 millilitres (½ pint) milk
300 millilitres (½ pint) water
2 eggs, beaten
Extra virgin olive oil
Caster sugar for dusting

Hot chocolate
175 grams (6 oz) plain chocolate
300 millilitres (½ pint) milk, boiling

Start by preparing the hot chocolate. Break chocolate into small pieces and place these in a heat-proof bowl that will fit snugly over a pan of simmering water. Fit bowl over simmering water and melt chocolate. As the chocolate begins to melt, stir in a little of the boiling milk until smooth and thick. Stir in the remaining milk, stirring constantly. Keep warm.

Sift flour on to a piece of greaseproof paper. Place milk and water in a saucepan and bring to boiling point. Tip in flour all at once, then stir until it forms a ball and comes away from the sides of the pan. Take pan off heat. Add eggs, stirring all the time until mixture is smooth.

In a thick-bottomed saucepan, heat olive oil until it begins to smoke. Fill a pastry bag fitted with a large round nozzle with churros dough. Squeeze long strips of dough into olive oil and fry until they are golden. With a slotted spoon, remove churros from oil and pat with kitchen paper to absorb excess oil. Dust with icing sugar and keep warm. To serve, pour hot chocolate into 2 warm mugs. Dunk churros into hot chocolate and eat. This is a popular Spanish breakfast dish.

Serves 2

MEXICAN CHICKEN MOLA

1 roasting chicken, 1.1–1.4 kilograms (2½–3 lbs)
1 carrot, chopped
1 onion, chopped
2 celery stalks, chopped
1 bay leaf
Salt
Water

Mola sauce
1 onion, chopped
2 cloves garlic, finely crushed
2 small hot green chillies, seeded and chopped
100–125 grams (4 oz) blanched almonds, chopped
50 grams (2 oz) seedless raisins
½ teaspoon coriander seeds
¼ teaspoon ground aniseed
1 slice toast
2 large tomatoes, stems removed
2–3 sprigs fresh coriander
½ teaspoon ground cinnamon
1 tablespoon lard
40 grams (1½ oz) bitter chocolate, grated
Salt and black pepper

Quarter chicken, carefully removing any lumps of fat from body cavity. Put chicken pieces in a pan with carrot, onion, celery stalks, bay leaf and just enough salted water to cover and cook gently, covered, until tender. This will take about 45 minutes.

Drain chicken pieces, reserving cooking liquor. Keep hot.
Strain cooking liquor and reserve 150 millilitres (¼ pint).
In an electric blender or food processor, combine onion,
chillies, almonds, raisins, coriander seeds, aniseed, toast,
tomatoes, coriander and cinnamon. Process to a purée.
In a large frying pan, heat the lard. Add purée and cook for
5 minutes, stirring all the time. Stir in reserved cooking
liquor, chocolate, and salt and pepper to taste, stirring until
chocolate has melted.
Return chicken pieces to pan and bring to simmering
point. Cook gently, covered, 15–20 minutes longer. Serve
immediately.

Serves 4

SPANISH PIGEONS IN CHOCOLATE

4 oven-ready pigeons, about 1.6 kilograms (4 lbs)
Salt and black pepper
65 grams (2½ oz) plain flour
50 millilitres (2 fl oz) extra virgin olive oil
16 pickling onions, peeled
3 cloves garlic, finely sliced
3 tablespoons dry white wine
75 millilitres (3 fl oz) chicken or game stock
15 grams (½ oz) dark chocolate, finely grated
Lemon wedges, for garnish

Wipe the pigeons with a damp cloth and season them inside and out with salt and black pepper. Place about 50 grams (2 oz) flour in a polythene bag and add the pigeons one by one. Shake the bag until each pigeon is well coated. Remove from the bag and shake off any excess.

In a heavy, flameproof casserole wide enough to take all the pigeons in one layer, heat olive oil, and brown birds on all sides. With a slotted spoon, take birds out of casserole. Add onions to casserole and push them around until they are browned on all sides. With a slotted spoon, take onions out of casserole.

Add garlic to casserole, and cook over a high heat for 1–2 minutes. Stir in remaining flour and cook for about 2 minutes. Add wine and stock and bring to boiling point, stirring constantly until the stock thickens.

Return pigeons to casserole and cover tightly. Simmer over a low heat for about 40 minutes. Add onions and salt and pepper to taste. Cover again and continue simmering for about 15 minutes until birds are cooked through.

Transfer pigeons and onions to a heated serving platter and keep hot. Skim any fat from cooking liquor in casserole. Stir in chocolate, and simmer, stirring until melted. Spoon sauce over pigeons and garnish platter with lemon wedges. Serve immediately.

Serves 4

FRUITY FONDUE

225 grams (8 oz) plain chocolate
150 millilitres (¼ pint) double cream
Pinch of grated nutmeg
½ teaspoon ground cloves
½ teaspoon ground cinnamon
Pinch of ground mixed spice
4 tablespoons Tia Maria, dark rum or brandy
Mixed fresh fruit pieces, to serve

Break chocolate into small pieces and place these in a fondue pot over a heat source. Add cream. Stir until chocolate and cream are thick and smooth. Stir in grated nutmeg, ground cloves, ground cinnamon and mixed spice, then stir in liqueur.

Keep sauce bubbling over a heat source. Serve with banana chunks, pineapple pieces, orange wedges and strawberries. Spear fruit with long-handled forks and dip in hot fondue sauce.

Serves 4

POIRES BELLE HÉLÈNE

6 juicy pears, peeled, halved, cored, poached and chilled
6 scoops vanilla ice cream

Bitter chocolate sauce
175 grams (6 oz) dark chocolate
40 grams (1½ oz) butter
150 millilitres (¼ pint) double cream
Vanilla essence, to taste

Start by preparing the sauce. Break chocolate into top of a double saucepan. Add butter and stir over simmering water until chocolate and butter are smooth. Beat in cream a little at a time. Place top part of pan over direct heat, bring sauce to boiling point, stirring all the time, and simmer, stirring, for 2–3 minutes. Remove from heat and flavour with a few drops of vanilla essence.

Drain pears and lightly pat them dry with kitchen paper. Put a scoop of ice cream in each of 6 glass dishes. Press half a pear to opposite sides of each scoop of ice cream, pointed ends up, and mask with warm chocolate sauce. Serve immediately.

Serves 6

CHOCOLATE-ORANGE MOUSSE

100–125 grams (4 oz) dark chocolate
25 grams (1 oz) unsalted butter
Finely grated rind and juice of 1 orange
1 tablespoon orange-flavoured liqueur
2 eggs, separated

Break chocolate into small pieces and place these in a heat-proof bowl that will fit snugly over a pan of simmering water. Add butter and orange rind and juice. Fit bowl over simmering water and melt chocolate and butter. Cool slightly and stir in orange liqueur.
In a bowl, whisk egg yolks until fluffy. Pour in chocolate mixture, whisking all the time. Whisk egg whites until stiff but not dry and fold into the chocolate mixture. Pour into 4 individual soufflé dishes; allow to become quite cold and chill until ready to serve.

Serves 4

HOT SOUFFLÉ

Butter and extra caster sugar for soufflé dish
50 grams (2 oz) caster sugar
75 grams (3 oz) plain chocolate
3 tablespoons brandy
2 tablespoons butter
1 tablespoon plain flour
150 millilitres (¼ pint) milk
3 eggs, separated
1 extra egg white
Cocoa powder, for dusting

Start by preparing soufflé dish. Grease bottom and insides of a 900 millilitre (1½ pint) soufflé dish. Coat insides of dish with caster sugar, then tip out excess.
Break chocolate into small pieces and place in a small heat-proof bowl that will fit snugly over a pan of simmering water. Place over simmering water and melt chocolate. Remove from heat, and stir in brandy.

Melt butter in a saucepan and stir in flour. Cook for 2 minutes, stirring all the time. Remove from heat, stir in milk, then bring to boiling point and simmer for 2 minutes, stirring until thick.

Remove pan from heat and stir in sugar, melted chocolate and egg yolks.

In a large bowl, beat egg whites until stiff but not dry. Using a large metal spoon, carefully fold egg whites into chocolate mixture. Spoon mixture into soufflé dish.

Bake soufflé in moderately hot oven (200°C, 400°F, Mark 6) for 35 minutes or until well risen. Remove from oven and quickly sift cocoa powder over top. Serve immediately.

Serves 4

THE QUEEN'S BAVAROIS

2 teaspoons unflavoured powdered gelatine
50 grams (2 oz) sugar
2 eggs, separated
300 millilitres (½ pint) milk
50 grams (2 oz) couverture chocolate
150 millilitres (¼ pint) double cream
Chocolate vermicelli and whipped cream for decoration

Sprinkle gelatine over 2 tablespoons cold water in a small cup. Then, when the gelatine has absorbed the water and set, stand the cup in a pan of hot water, stirring until the liquid is clear. Allow to cool to room temperature.

In a large heat-proof bowl that will fit snugly over a pan of simmering water, whisk the egg yolks and sugar together until light, fluffy and almost white. Put milk and chocolate in a thick-bottomed saucepan and bring to boiling point, stirring until chocolate is melted. Off the heat, pour gradually into the egg yolks and sugar, whisking all the time. Fit bowl over simmering water and cook, stirring until custard is thick enough to coat back of spoon. Take care not to let it boil, or egg yolks will curdle.

Remove from heat and stir in gelatine mixture. Pour through a strainer into a clean bowl. Leave until quite cold, stirring occasionally.

Whisk egg whites to a firm snow. In another bowl, whisk cream until thick and floppy but not stiff. With a large metal spoon, fold cream into chocolate mixture, followed by egg whites. Spoon into a well-greased mould. Chill for several hours in refrigerator.

Serve unmoulded and decorated with whipped cream and chocolate vermicelli.

Serves 6–8

TRUFFLE AND HAZELNUT RING

750 millilitres (1½ pints) single cream
200 grams (7 oz) caster sugar
7 egg yolks, lightly beaten
100–125 grams (4 oz) cocoa powder
175 millilitres (6 fl oz) whipping cream
175 grams (6 oz) plain chocolate, chopped
4 tablespoons nut liqueur
1 tablespoon orange-flavoured liqueur
25 grams (1 oz) toasted hazelnuts, chopped
Whipped cream and chocolate curls, for decoration

In a thick-bottomed saucepan, gently heat cream and sugar together, stirring until sugar dissolves. Bring almost to boiling point, then take off heat and allow to cool for 5 minutes.

Place eggs in a large bowl and gradually pour cream on to eggs, whisking all the time. Strain mixture into rinsed-out saucepan and heat very gently over low heat, until custard is creamy and stays separated if you run your finger through it on the back of a wooden spoon. Take care not to let it boil, or egg yolks will curdle.

Take off heat and stir in cocoa. Leave until quite cold, stirring occasionally. Pour custard into a freezer-proof container, cover and freeze until solid around edges.

Place whipping cream and chocolate in a small saucepan over low heat, stirring until chocolate melts. Take off heat and stir in liqueurs and hazelnuts. Allow to cool completely.

Line bottom of a 1.2 litre (2 pint) ring mould with three-quarters of chocolate ice cream. With a small spoon, push ice cream up sides of mould to form a deep groove in centre. Place in freezer for a few minutes to firm. Pour cream and hazelnut mixture into groove, then cover with remaining ice cream. Cover and freeze until firm.

Transfer to the main compartment of refrigerator about 30 minutes before serving. Decorate with whipped cream and chocolate curls just before serving.

Serves 8—10

MINTY CHOCOLATE ICE CREAM

---

50 grams (2 oz) caster sugar
3 egg yolks
300 millilitres (½ pint) single cream
300 millilitres (½ pint) double cream
6 tablespoons crème de menthe
100–125 grams (4 oz) dark chocolate, coarsely chopped

In a thick-bottomed saucepan, dissolve the sugar in 125 millilitres (4 fl oz) water. Place a sugar thermometer in the water. Bring to boiling point and boil until a temperature of 90°C (194°F) is reached.

In a large bowl, beat egg yolks. Pour sugar syrup on to egg yolks, beating all the time until mixture is thick and light.

In another large bowl, beat creams together until soft peaks form. With a large metal spoon, fold into the egg yolk mixture, followed by crème de menthe and chocolate pieces.

Transfer to an ice cube tray or shallow plastic box. Cover and freeze until firm. Transfer to the main compartment of refrigerator about 30 minutes before serving.

Serves 6

DOUBLE CHOCOLATE CHIP COOKIES

---

175 grams (6 oz) butter, room temperature
90 grams (3½ oz) caster sugar
200 grams (7 oz) light soft brown sugar
1 teaspoon vanilla essence
2 eggs, lightly beaten
200 grams (7 oz) plain flour
25 grams (1 oz) cocoa powder
1 teaspoon bicarbonate of soda
1 teaspoon salt
300 grams (10 oz) plain chocolate chips
Butter for baking tray

Cream butter, caster sugar, brown sugar and vanilla essence together until light and fluffy. Add eggs and beat well. Sift flour, cocoa powder, bicarbonate of soda and salt together on to the creamed mixture. Beat together, then beat in chocolate chips.

Drop the mixture in mounds on a well-buttered baking tray. Bake in a moderate oven (190°C, 375°F, Mark 5) for 8–10 minutes, until cookies are firm to the touch. (You will have to make in several batches.) Allow to cool on baking tray for a few minutes, then use a round-bladed knife to transfer to the rack to cool. Store in an air-tight container.

Makes about 60 cookies

TRADITIONAL BROWNIES

100–125 grams (4 oz) plain chocolate
100–125 grams (4 oz) butter, diced
100–125 grams (4 oz) soft brown sugar
100–125 grams (4 oz) self-raising flour
Pinch of salt
2 eggs, lightly beaten
75 grams (3 oz) walnuts, chopped
1 ½ tablespoons milk
Butter for cake tin

Break chocolate into small pieces and place these in a heat-proof bowl that will fit snugly over a pan of simmering water. Add butter. Fit bowl over simmering water and melt chocolate and butter. Stir until smooth. Remove from heat. Stir in sugar and beat until well combined. Allow to cool.

Sift flour and salt into a bowl, and make a well in the centre. Pour in cooled chocolate. Beat, gradually drawing in flour from the sides. Beat in eggs, walnuts and milk to make a soft dropping consistency.

Pour into a well-buttered 20 centimetre (8 in.) square cake tin. Bake in a moderate oven (180°C, 350°F, Mark 4) for 30 minutes until a skewer pushed right down to the bottom through the middle comes out clean and dry. Allow brownies to cool in tin before cutting into 16 squares.

Makes 16

DARK DATE CAKE

3 tablespoons plain flour
2 tablespoons unsweetened cocoa powder
1 teaspoon baking powder
4 eggs, separated
225 grams (8 oz) caster sugar
1–2 tablespoons fresh orange juice
175 grams (6 oz) stoned dried dates, chopped
175 grams (6 oz) walnuts, chopped
Pinch of salt
Butter for cake tin
300 millilitres (½ pint) double cream

Sift flour with cocoa and baking powder. Beat egg yolks and sugar together until thick and fluffy. Beat in 1 tablespoon orange juice. Sift flour and cocoa mixture again over the surface, and with a large metal spoon, lightly fold it in, together with a little more orange juice if necessary to make a light, creamy batter. Fold in chopped dates and walnuts until mixed.

Beat egg whites with a pinch of salt until stiff but not dry.
Gently fold into cake batter. Immediately spoon batter into
a well-buttered 22.5 centimetre (9 in.) tubular cake tin.
Bake in a slow oven (170°C, 325°F, Mark 3) until cake is
well risen, lightly coloured on top and has shrunk away
slightly from sides of tin. This will take 35–40 minutes. ·
Allow cake to 'settle' for 15 minutes before turning out on
a wire rack. Leave until quite cold before covering with
lightly sweetened whipped cream.

Serves 6–8

CITRUS PECAN CAKE

100–125 grams pecans, finely ground
3 tablespoons plain flour
1 tablespoon baking powder
Generous pinch of salt
Finely grated rind of 1 orange
Juice of ½ orange
4 eggs, separated
150 grams (5 oz) caster sugar
3 tablespoons melted butter
Pecan halves, to decorate

Chocolate icing
100–125 grams (4 oz) dark chocolate
2 tablespoons melted butter

Mix the ground nuts with the flour, baking powder, salt and orange rind. Beat the egg yolks until thick and lemon-coloured, then gradually beat in 90 grams (3½ oz) sugar.
Fold in walnut mixture, followed by orange juice.
Whisk egg whites until they form soft, floppy peaks. Gradually add remaining sugar, whisking constantly to make a stiff meringue. Fold meringue into yolk mixture.
Spoon cake mixture into a well-buttered, deep 20 centimetre (8 in.) cake tin. Bake in a moderate oven (180°C, 350°F, Mark 4) for 40 minutes. Allow cake to cool in its tin on a rack for 10 minutes before turning it out on to the rack and leaving it until cold.

To make chocolate icing, break the chocolate into small pieces and place these in a heat-proof bowl that will fit snugly over a pan of simmering water and leave until chocolate has melted, stirring frequently. Stir in butter and beat until smooth. Spread icing over cake top and sides. Decorate with pecan halves.

Serves 4–6

CAROB CREATIONS

75 grams (3 oz) plain carob
50 grams (2 oz) butter
100–125 grams (4 oz) soft light brown sugar
75 grams (3 oz) plain flour
½ teaspoon baking powder
1 egg, beaten
1 teaspoon vanilla essence
½ teaspoon salt
40 grams (1½ oz) walnut halves, chopped
Butter for cake tin

Break carob into small pieces and place these in a heat-proof bowl that will fit snugly over a pan of simmering water with butter and sugar. Fit bowl over simmering water and melt chocolate and butter. Take off heat.

Sift flour and baking powder on to melted chocolate mixture. Add remaining ingredients and mix well.

Spoon into a well-buttered 20 centimetre (8 in.) square cake tin. Bake in a moderate oven (180°C, 350°F, Mark 4) for 15 minutes until slightly risen and shiny on top. Allow to cool in tin.

To serve, cut into 5 centimetre (2 in.) bars. Store in an air-tight container.

Makes 16 bars

STRAWBERRY QUAKE

900 grams (2 lbs) strawberries, hulled and puréed
700 grams (1 ½ lb) sugar
Butter for baking tray
450 grams (1 lb) couverture chocolate

Place strawberry purée in a thick-bottomed saucepan. Stir in sugar. Cook over a low heat, stirring all the time until mixture is thick enough for a clean line to be left on bottom of pan when a spoon is drawn across it. Remove pan from heat.

Distribute mixture in about 24 little mounds on a well-buttered baking tray. Leave to set.

When each strawberry jelly is firm to touch, prepare the chocolate coating. Break chocolate into small pieces and place in small heat-proof bowl that will fit snugly over a pan of simmering water. Place over simmering water and melt chocolate. Beat until smooth and creamy. Place a sugar thermometer in the chocolate and leave until temperature has fallen to 43°C (110 °F).

Line a baking tray with waxed paper. Drop jellies, one at a time, into chocolate. Lift out with a fork and slide on to baking tray. Leave for several hours until chocolate is completely hard. Store between pieces of waxed paper in an air-tight container.

Makes about 24

CARNIVAL IN RIO

450 grams (1 lb) Brazil nuts, shelled
450 grams (1 lb) couverture chocolate

Put the nuts on a baking tray and roast in a slow oven (170°C, 325°F, Mark 3) until the skins become flaky. Peel off skins, wash nuts and dry on kitchen paper. Break chocolate into small pieces and place these in a heat-proof bowl that will fit snugly over a pan of simmering water. Fit bowl over simmering water and melt chocolate. Use a sugar thermometer to check the temperature of the chocolate. It should never exceed 49°C (120 °F). When the chocolate has melted completely, stir until the consistency is creamy and smooth.

Place the sugar thermometer in the chocolate and leave until the temperature has fallen to 43°C (110°F). Place the nuts on a tray by the side of the bowl. Line another tray with bakewell paper. Drop one nut at a time into the melted chocolate. Lift out on a fork, tapping the fork on the side of the bowl to remove excess chocolate. Slide chocolate Brazil nuts on to tray lined with bakewell paper. Leave for about an hour, until the chocolate is completely hard, before eating.

Makes 450 grams
(1 lb)

ITALIAN GAME SAUCE

2 tablespoons brown sugar
4 tablespoons currants
100–125 grams (4 oz) dark chocolate, grated
1 tablespoon chopped candied orange peel
1 tablespoon chopped candied lemon peel
250 millilitres (8 fl oz) red wine vinegar
1 tablespoon capers
1 tablespoon pine nuts

Place brown sugar, currants, grated chocolate, candied orange and lemon peels, red wine vinegar and capers in a saucepan. Allow to soak for 2 hours.

Simmer sauce for 2 minutes, stirring occasionally. Stir in pine nut just before serving. Serve with game, grilled turkey drumsticks or braised rabbit.

Serves 4

RICH FUDGE SAUCE

100–125 grams (4 oz) plain chocolate
100–125 grams (4 oz) butter, diced
100–125 grams (4 oz) light soft brown sugar
100–125 grams (4 oz) caster sugar
300 millilitres (½ pint) evaporated milk

Break chocolate into a thick-bottomed saucepan. Add butter and light soft brown and caster sugars. Place pan over medium heat and stir until chocolate is melted and sugars dissolved. Stir in milk. Bring sauce to boiling point, stirring constantly, and simmer, stirring, for 5 minutes. Remove from heat.

Serve sauce hot or warm with ice creams, frozen yogurts, pancakes or hot puddings.

Serves 4

BUTTERCREAM ICING

100–125 grams (4 oz) plain chocolate
4 egg yolks
100–125 grams (4 oz) caster sugar
225 grams (8 oz) butter, room temperature
2–3 teaspoons vanilla essence

Break chocolate into small pieces and place these in a heat-proof bowl that will fit snugly over a pan of simmering water. Fit bowl over simmering water and melt chocolate, stirring until smooth. Remove from heat and allow to cool until just beginning to set.

Whisk egg yolks. In thick-bottomed saucepan, heat sugar gently with 90 millilitres (3½ fl oz) water, stirring until dissolved. Bring to boiling point. Use a sugar thermometer to check the temperature of syrup. It should reach 115°C (240 °F). Remove from heat.

Whisking constantly, pour syrup on to egg yolks in steady stream. Whisk until cool, pale and mousse-like.

Cream butter until it is same consistency as yolk mixture. Beat it gradually into yolks. Stir in cooled chocolate and vanilla essence.

CAROB SMOOTHIE

1.1 litres (2 pints) milk
3 tablespoons molasses
3 tablespoons carob powder
1 ripe banana, peeled
50 grams (2 oz) shelled peanuts, finely ground

Put all the ingredients in an electric blender or food processor and whirl until smooth and creamy. Serve in tall, chilled glasses.

Serves 4

FROTHY MILKSHAKE

4 tablespoons chocolate syrup
350 millilitres (12 fl oz) milk, chilled
2 teaspoons sugar
1 teaspoon vanilla essence
225 grams (8 oz) vanilla ice cream
whipped cream, to serve

Place chocolate syrup, milk, sugar and vanilla essence in an electric blender or food processor. Whirl until frothy. Add ice cream and whirl again.

Pour frothy milkshakes into tall glasses. Top each with whipped cream. Serve immediately.

Serves 2–3

MEASUREMENTS

Quantities have been given in both metric and imperial measures in this book. However, many foodstuffs are now available only in metric quantities; the list below gives metric measures for weight and liquid capacity, and their imperial equivalents used in this book.

WEIGHT

25 grams	1 oz
50 grams	2 oz
75 grams	3 oz
100 – 125 grams	4 oz
150 grams	5 oz
175 grams	6 oz
200 grams	7 oz
225 grams	8 oz
250 grams	9 oz
275 grams	10 oz
300 grams	11 oz
350 grams	12 oz
375 grams	13 oz

400 grams	14 oz
425 grams	15 oz
450 grams	1 lb
500 grams (½ kilogram)	1 lb 1½ oz
1 kilogram	2 lb 3 oz
1.5 kilograms	3 lb 5 oz
2 kilograms	4 lb 6 oz
2.5 kilograms	5 lb 8 oz
3 kilograms	6 lb 10 oz
3.5 kilograms	7 lb 11 oz
4 kilograms	8 lb 13 oz
4.5 kilograms	9 lb 14 oz
5 kilograms	11 lb

LIQUID CAPACITY

150 millilitres	¼ pint
300 millilitres	½ pint
425 millilitres	¾ pint
550 – 600 millilitres	1 pint
900 millilitres	1½ pints
1000 millilitres (1 litre)	1¾ pints
1.2 litres	2 pints
1.3 litres	2¼ pints
1.4 litres	2½ pints
1.5 litres	2¾ pints
1.9 litres	3¼ pints
2 litres	3½ pints
2.5 litres	4½ pints

OVEN TEMPERATURES

Very low	130°C, 250°F, Mark ½
Low	140°C, 275°F, Mark 1
Very slow	150°C, 300°F, Mark 2
Slow	170°C, 325°F, Mark 3
Moderate	180°C, 350°F, Mark 4
	190°C, 375°F, Mark 5
Moderately hot	200°C, 400°F, Mark 6
Fairly hot	220°C, 425°F, Mark 7
Hot	230°C, 450°F, Mark 8